What We Have in Common

A Brim Coloring Book

Written by Jane Landey
Edited by David Austin
Drawings by David Austin and Jane Austin

Published by CreateSpace: An Amazon Company.
Printed in U.S.A.

Introduction

What We Have in Common. Brim Coloring Books enable children to color the drawings as they read along! The books display the similarities of related animals. In this series, the kangaroo and the wallaby are compared. The facts enable children to appreciate common values. Thus, imbibing in them interest towards animals which could help them appreciate what they have in common with one another.

THE KANGAROO

AND

THE WALLABY

The kangaroo and the wallaby have many things in common.
They look alike and both carry their young ones in their pouches. Both live on grassy land.

A kangaroo and a wallaby meet
on a grassy land.

I am a kangaroo.

I am a wallaby.

I have a muscular tail.

I have a strong tail too!

And I have long pointed ears.

I have long pointed ears too!

I like to eat flowers.

I love to eat grasses and plants too!

I hop. Do you?

Yes I do and skip too!

I live in mobs.

I live in herds!

I carry my baby in my pouch.

I carry my baby in my pouch too!

And I feed my baby with milk.

I feed my baby with milk too!

I can stamp my feet.

I can too!

I also box and kick.

So do I!

Do you want to box?

No, I do not want to box!

Why?

You are stronger than me!

Alright, let us look for some good plants!

That is a good idea!

Are you ready?

Yes I am!

Go that way and I go this way.

Sure!

Bye!

Bye!

What We Have in Common Brim Coloring Books

Crocodile and Alligator
Turtle and Tortoise
Starfish and Octopus
Worm and Snake
Turkey and Vulture
Ostrich and Emu
Weka and Kiwi
Bat and Rat
Camel and Llama
Duck and Pelican
Kangaroo and Wallaby
Pig and Tapir
Skunk and Squirrel
Hedge and Anteater
Cat and Owl
Elephant and Rhinoceros
Dog and Fox
Buffalo and Bull
Leopard and Cheetah
Horse and Zebra